P9-CFO-700

She
Believed
She Could
So She
Did

summersdale

SHE BELIEVED SHE COULD SO SHE DID

An Hachette UK Company
www.hachette.co.uk

Summersdale Publishers Ltd
Part of Octopus Publishing Group Limited
Carmelite House
50 Victoria Embankment
LONDON
EC4Y 0DZ
UK

www.summersdale.com

Printed and bound in the Czech Republic

ISBN: 978-1-78685-488-9

Substantial discounts on bulk quantities of Summersdale books are available to corporations, professional associations and other organisations. For details contact general enquiries: telephone: +44 (0) 1243 771107 or email: enquiries@summersdale.com.

TO............................

FROM ....

A GIRL SHOULD
BE TWO THINGS:
WHO AND WHAT
SHE WANTS.

Coco Chanel

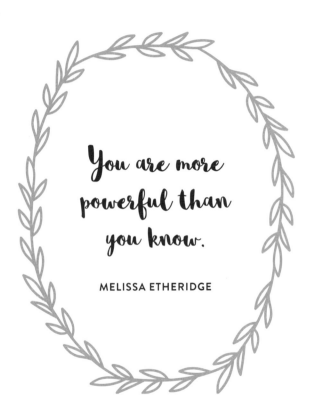

You are more powerful than you know.

MELISSA ETHERIDGE

WE HAVE TO
DARE TO BE
OURSELVES,
HOWEVER
FRIGHTENING
OR STRANGE
THAT SELF MAY
PROVE TO BE.

May Sarton

Be the girl
who decided to
go for it

ONE IS NOT BORN, BUT RATHER BECOMES, A WOMAN.

Simone de Beauvoir

WE MUST BELIEVE WE ARE
GIFTED FOR SOMETHING
AND THAT THIS THING, AT
WHATEVER COST, MUST
BE MAINTAINED.

MARIE CURIE

You have to have confidence in your ability, and then be tough enough to follow through.

ROSALYNN CARTER

Treasure
your
successes

IF YOU DON'T
RISK ANYTHING,
YOU RISK
EVEN MORE.

Erica Jong

I DON'T FOCUS ON
WHAT I'M UP AGAINST.
I FOCUS ON MY
GOALS AND I TRY TO
IGNORE THE REST.

VENUS WILLIAMS

ABOVE ALL,
BE THE HEROINE
OF YOUR LIFE.

Nora Ephron

Be a girl with
a mind, a woman
with attitude and
a lady with class

I want to
encourage women
to embrace their
own uniqueness.

MIRANDA KERR

THE
EXCITEMENT
OF DREAMS
COMING TRUE
IS BEYOND THE
DESCRIPTION
OF WORDS.

LAILAH GIFTY AKITA

The best way to make
your dreams come
true is to wake up.

PAUL VALÉRY

Self-belief is
the highest form
of power

BELIEF IN
ONESELF IS ONE
OF THE MOST
IMPORTANT BRICKS
IN BUILDING ANY
SUCCESSFUL
VENTURE.

Lydia Maria Child

WIN OR LOSE,
ONLY I HOLD
THE KEY TO
MY DESTINY.

ELAINE MAXWELL

IF YOU THINK
TAKING CARE
OF YOURSELF
IS SELFISH,
CHANGE
YOUR MIND.

Ann Richards

Girls with
dreams become
women with
vision

MAKE THE MOST
OF YOURSELF BY
FANNING THE TINY,
INNER SPARKS
OF POSSIBILITY
INTO FLAMES OF
ACHIEVEMENT.

Golda Meir

A woman is
the full circle.
Within her is the
power to create,
nurture and
transform.

DIANE MARIECHILD

THE THINGS YOU ARE PASSIONATE ABOUT ARE NOT RANDOM, THEY ARE YOUR CALLING.

Fabienne Fredrickson

ALL GREAT ACHIEVEMENTS REQUIRE TIME.

Maya Angelou

NEVER GROW A
WISHBONE, DAUGHTER,
WHERE YOUR BACKBONE
OUGHT TO BE.

CLEMENTINE PADDLEFORD

A CHARMING WOMAN DOESN'T FOLLOW THE CROWD. SHE IS HERSELF.

LORETTA YOUNG

Be your
own kind
of beautiful

THE ROUGHEST
ROAD OFTEN LEADS
TO THE TOP.

Christina Aguilera

THE MOST ALLURING THING A WOMAN CAN HAVE IS CONFIDENCE.

BEYONCÉ

THE DIFFERENCE BETWEEN SUCCESSFUL PEOPLE AND OTHERS IS HOW LONG THEY SPEND FEELING SORRY FOR THEMSELVES.

Barbara Corcoran

Girls

support girls

Success is
a state of mind.
If you want success,
start thinking
of yourself as
a success.

JOYCE BROTHERS

TAKING JOY IN LIVING IS A WOMAN'S BEST COSMETIC.

ROSALIND RUSSELL

If you ask me what
I came into this life to
do, I will tell you: I
came to live out loud.

ÉMILE ZOLA

Be a princess.
Be a nerd.
Be a warrior.
Above all,
be you.

I'm not
afraid of storms,
for I'm learning
how to sail
my ship.

LOUISA MAY ALCOTT

I AM MY
OWN WOMAN.

EVA PERÓN

THERE IS ALWAYS
A REALISTIC WAY
TO FULFIL ANY
DREAM. THERE
HAS NEVER BEEN
A DREAM THAT
YOU CAN'T HAVE.

Barbara Sher

Let them watch you rise

THE ONLY POWER
THAT EXISTS
IS INSIDE
OURSELVES.

Anne Rice

Only do
what your heart
tells you.

DIANA, PRINCESS OF WALES

THE BEST
PROTECTION
ANY WOMAN
CAN HAVE...
IS COURAGE.

Elizabeth Cady Stanton

You can rule
the world; just
don't be afraid to
wear the crown

THINK LIKE
A QUEEN.
A QUEEN IS NOT
AFRAID TO FAIL.
FAILURE IS
ANOTHER
STEPPING STONE
TO GREATNESS.

Oprah Winfrey

I ALWAYS DID
SOMETHING I WAS
A LITTLE NOT
READY TO DO.

MARISSA MAYER

I am not
a has-been.
I am a will be.

LAUREN BACALL

She looks
to the future
and smiles

A STRONG
WOMAN LOOKS
A CHALLENGE
DEAD IN THE
EYE AND GIVES
IT A WINK.

Gina Carey

DON'T COMPROMISE YOURSELF. YOU'RE ALL YOU'VE GOT.

JANIS JOPLIN

I SAY IF
I'M BEAUTIFUL.
I SAY IF
I'M STRONG.
YOU WILL NOT
DETERMINE MY
STORY – I WILL.

Amy Schumer

The future belongs
to those who believe
in the beauty of
their dreams.

ELEANOR ROOSEVELT

I LOVE TO
SEE A YOUNG
GIRL GO OUT
AND GRAB THE
WORLD BY
THE LAPELS.

MAYA ANGELOU

We ask ourselves, 'Who am I to be brilliant, gorgeous, talented, fabulous?' Actually, who are you not to be?

MARIANNE WILLIAMSON

You are the girl
that you know
yourself to be

A LOT OF
PEOPLE ARE
AFRAID TO SAY
WHAT THEY WANT.
THAT'S WHY THEY
DON'T GET WHAT
THEY WANT.

Madonna

YOUR VICTORY IS RIGHT AROUND THE CORNER. NEVER GIVE UP.

NICKI MINAJ

A WOMAN WITH A VOICE IS, BY DEFINITION, A STRONG WOMAN.

Melinda Gates

You can never
be overdressed
or overeducated

THE SUCCESS OF
EVERY WOMAN
SHOULD BE THE
INSPIRATION
TO ANOTHER.

Serena Williams

There can be
no happiness if the
things we believe
in are different
from the things
we do.

FREYA STARK

DON'T LIVE DOWN
TO EXPECTATIONS.
GO OUT THERE AND
DO SOMETHING
REMARKABLE.

Wendy Wasserstein

Don't be
afraid to take the
first step, no matter
what shoes
you wear

WE DON'T
RECOGNISE OUR
OWN BEAUTY
BECAUSE WE'RE
TOO BUSY
COMPARING
OURSELVES TO
OTHER PEOPLE.

Kelly Osbourne

WE MAY ENCOUNTER
MANY DEFEATS,
BUT WE MUST NOT
BE DEFEATED.

MAYA ANGELOU

THERE IS NO FORCE EQUAL TO A WOMAN DETERMINED TO RISE.

W. E. B. DU BOIS

Take up all the space you need - this is your world too

WOMEN MUST TRY
TO DO THINGS AS
MEN HAVE TRIED.
WHEN THEY FAIL,
THEIR FAILURE
MUST BE BUT
A CHALLENGE
TO OTHERS.

Amelia Earhart

ENERGY RIGHTLY
APPLIED AND
DIRECTED WILL
ACCOMPLISH
ANYTHING.

NELLIE BLY

DEFINE SUCCESS
ON YOUR OWN
TERMS, ACHIEVE
IT BY YOUR OWN
RULES, AND BUILD
A LIFE YOU'RE
PROUD TO LIVE.

Anne Sweeney

She needed
a hero so
that's what
she became

If we stop defining each other by what we are not and start defining ourselves by what we are, we can all be freer.

EMMA WATSON

UNIQUE AND DIFFERENT IS THE NEXT GENERATION OF BEAUTIFUL.

TAYLOR SWIFT

Without leaps
of imagination or
dreaming, we lose
the excitement of
possibilities. Dreaming,
after all, is a form
of planning.

GLORIA STEINEM

Fight like
a girl

You can be strong
and true to yourself
without being
rude or loud.

PAULA RADCLIFFE

JUST BE YOURSELF – THERE IS NO ONE BETTER.

TAYLOR SWIFT

OPTIMISM CAN BE RELEARNT.

Marian Keyes

You can,
you shall and
you will

BELIEVE IN
YOURSELF AND
YOU CAN ACHIEVE
GREATNESS IN
YOUR LIFE.

Judy Blume

Find something you're passionate about and keep tremendously interested in it.

JULIA CHILD

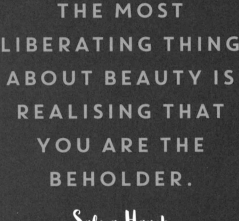

THE MOST
LIBERATING THING
ABOUT BEAUTY IS
REALISING THAT
YOU ARE THE
BEHOLDER.

Salma Hayek

Remain strong when things go wrong

I NEVER LOSE SIGHT OF THE FACT THAT JUST BEING IS FUN.

Katharine Hepburn

DO WHAT YOU HAVE
TO DO UNTIL YOU
CAN DO WHAT YOU
WANT TO DO.

OPRAH WINFREY

To the doubters
and naysayers -
Your resistance
made me stronger,
made me push harder.

MADONNA

You can do anything you put your mind to

I WAS SMART
ENOUGH TO
GO THROUGH
ANY DOOR
THAT OPENED.

Joan Rivers

GOALS ARE DREAMS WITH DEADLINES.

DIANA SCHARF-HUNT

KNOW WHAT YOU WANT AND REACH OUT EAGERLY FOR IT.

Lailah Gifty Akita

Learn to
dance in
the rain

Just don't give up trying to do what you really want to do. Where there is love and inspiration, I don't think you can go wrong.

ELLA FITZGERALD

WE NEED
TO GET THE
MESSAGE OUT
THAT YOU ARE
VALUED, YOU
ARE A GODDESS
AND DON'T
FORGET THAT.

JENNIFER LOPEZ

When you have
a dream, you've
got to grab it and
never let go.

CAROL BURNETT

Get it, girl

WOMEN ARE
THE LARGEST
UNTAPPED
RESERVOIR
OF TALENT IN
THE WORLD.

Hillary Clinton

SHE STOOD IN THE
STORM, AND WHEN THE
WIND DID NOT BLOW HER
WAY... SHE ADJUSTED
HER SAILS.

ELIZABETH EDWARDS

THE MERE FACT
OF BEING ABLE
TO CALL YOUR
JOB YOUR
PASSION IS
SUCCESS IN
MY EYES.

Alicia Vikander

Dream
Believe
Achieve

A GREAT PART
OF COURAGE IS
THE COURAGE OF
HAVING DONE THE
THING BEFORE.

Ralph Waldo Emerson

Age cannot wither her, nor custom stale her infinite variety.

WILLIAM SHAKESPEARE

THE QUESTION ISN'T WHO IS GOING TO LET ME; IT'S WHO IS GOING TO STOP ME.

Ayn Rand

Book the ticket
Write the book
Live the dream

IT TOOK
ME QUITE
A LONG TIME
TO DEVELOP A
VOICE, AND NOW
THAT I HAVE IT,
I AM NOT GOING
TO BE SILENT.

Madeleine Albright

A STRONG, POSITIVE
SELF-IMAGE IS THE BEST
POSSIBLE PREPARATION
FOR SUCCESS.

JOYCE BROTHERS

YOU HAVE
WHAT IT
TAKES TO BE
A VICTORIOUS,
INDEPENDENT,
FEARLESS
WOMAN.

TYRA BANKS

Live

Laugh

Love

I BELIEVE IN
WRITING YOUR
OWN STORY.

Charlotte Eriksson

THERE ARE TWO WAYS
OF SPREADING LIGHT:
TO BE THE CANDLE
OR THE MIRROR
THAT REFLECTS IT.

EDITH WHARTON

THE BEST AND
MOST BEAUTIFUL
THINGS IN THE
WORLD CANNOT
BE SEEN NOR
EVEN TOUCHED,
BUT JUST FELT
IN THE HEART.

Helen Keller

Dive head
first into every
challenge

I learned to always take on things I'd never done before. Growth and comfort do not coexist.

GINNI ROMETTY

GINGER ROGERS DID EVERYTHING (FRED ASTAIRE) DID... BACKWARDS AND IN HIGH HEELS.

BOB THAVES

Tell me, what is it
you plan to do
with your one wild
and precious life?

MARY OLIVER

Life is a
risk worth
taking

The truth is,
I often like women.
I like their
unconventionality.
I like their
completeness. I like
their anonymity.

VIRGINIA WOOLF

YOU MUST DO THE THING YOU THINK YOU CANNOT DO.

ELEANOR ROOSEVELT

THROW CAUTION TO THE WIND AND JUST DO IT.

Carrie Underwood

Live for
yourself,
no one else

THE MOST
DIFFICULT THING
IS THE DECISION TO
ACT. THE REST IS
MERELY TENACITY.

Amelia Earhart

If you don't
like the road
you're walking,
start paving
another one.

DOLLY PARTON

IF YOU REALLY
WANT TO FLY,
JUST HARNESS
YOUR POWER TO
YOUR PASSION.

Oprah Winfrey

Don't lose
your fire

YOU HAVE TO
BE STRONG AND
COURAGEOUS
AND KNOW THAT
YOU CAN DO
ANYTHING YOU
PUT YOUR
MIND TO.

Leah LaBelle

ALWAYS BE A FIRST-RATE
VERSION OF YOURSELF,
INSTEAD OF A
SECOND-RATE VERSION
OF SOMEONE ELSE.

JUDY GARLAND

Just when the
caterpillar thought
the world was
ending, it became
a butterfly.

PROVERB

Rules
don't apply

I FEEL THERE
IS SOMETHING
UNEXPLORED
ABOUT WOMEN
THAT ONLY A
WOMAN CAN
EXPLORE.

Georgia O'Keeffe

THERE IS NO LIMIT
TO WHAT WE, AS
WOMEN, CAN
ACCOMPLISH.

MICHELLE OBAMA

WHATEVER
I DID, I DID.
MY MISTAKES
ARE MINE.
I, ALONE, AM
RESPONSIBLE.

Bette Davis

Trust your
inner voice:
she is a goddess
talking to you

You shouldn't go through life with a catcher's mitt on both hands; you need to be able to throw something back.

MAYA ANGELOU

I DO
NOT KNOW
ANYONE WHO
HAS GOT TO THE
TOP WITHOUT
HARD WORK.

MARGARET THATCHER

To succeed you
have to believe in
something with such
a passion that it
becomes a reality.

ANITA RODDICK

A flower does not
compete with the
blossoms next to it –
it just blooms

BEAUTY IS
PERFECT IN ITS
IMPERFECTIONS,
SO YOU JUST HAVE
TO GO WITH THE
IMPERFECTIONS.

Diane von Fürstenberg

TAKE CRITICISM SERIOUSLY, BUT NOT PERSONALLY.

HILLARY CLINTON

FAR AWAY IN THE
SUNSHINE ARE MY
HIGHEST ASPIRATIONS.
I MAY NOT REACH
THEM, BUT I CAN LOOK
UP AND SEE THEIR
BEAUTY, BELIEVE IN
THEM, AND TRY TO
FOLLOW WHERE
THEY LEAD.

Louisa May Alcott

You are valuable
You are powerful
You are deserving

YOU CAN
NEVER LEAVE
FOOTPRINTS THAT
LAST IF YOU ARE
ALWAYS WALKING
ON TIPTOE.

Leymah Gbowee

We must have
perseverance and
above all
confidence
in ourselves.

MARIE CURIE

THE WORLD
YOU DESIRE
CAN BE WON.
IT EXISTS...
IT IS REAL...
IT IS POSSIBLE...
IT IS YOURS.

Ayn Rand

Adventure
awaits those
who seek it

DO ONE THING EVERY DAY THAT SCARES YOU.

Mary Schmich

WE ARE
THE HERO OF OUR
OWN STORY.

MARY McCARTHY

THE MOST
EFFECTIVE WAY
TO DO IT IS
TO DO IT.

AMELIA EARHART

Kindness
is courage

NOTHING IS IMPOSSIBLE; THE WORD ITSELF SAYS 'I'M POSSIBLE'!

Audrey Hepburn

I CAN'T THINK OF ANY
BETTER REPRESENTATION
OF BEAUTY THAN SOMEONE
WHO IS UNAFRAID
TO BE HERSELF.

EMMA STONE

I DWELL IN
POSSIBILITY.

Emily Dickinson

You are a
diamond - never
let them dull
your sparkle

Never give up,
for that is just the
place and time that
the tide will turn.

HARRIET BEECHER STOWE

SUCCESS IS ONLY MEANINGFUL AND ENJOYABLE IF IT FEELS LIKE YOUR OWN.

MICHELLE OBAMA

I used to want the words 'She tried' on my tombstone. Now I want 'She did it'.

KATHERINE DUNHAM

She believed
she could
so she did

If you're interested in finding out more about our books, find us on Facebook at **Summersdale Publishers** and follow us on Twitter at **@Summersdale**.

www.summersdale.com

Image credits

pp.1, 7, 19, 27, 39, 47, 67, 79, 99, 107, 119, 139, 147, 159 © Rolau Elena/Shutterstock.com

pp.3, 11, 23, 31, 43, 51, 59, 63, 71, 83, 87, 91, 103, 111, 123, 131, 143, 151 © handini_atmodiwiryo/Shutterstock.com

pp.5, 25, 45, 85, 105, 125, 145
© mhatzapa/Shutterstock.com

pp.6, 9, 14, 21, 26, 29, 34, 46, 49, 54, 61, 66, 69, 74, 86, 89, 94, 101, 106, 109, 114, 126, 129, 134, 141, 146, 149, 154, 160 © Alenka Karabanova/Shutterstock.com

pp.17, 30, 37, 57, 70, 77, 97, 110, 117, 137, 150, 157 – leaves © NIKHOMKEDBAN/Shutterstock.com